Oddball eYeballs

A book on vision and how weird it is

by the editors of
KLUTZ

KLUTZ

is a kids' company staffed entirely by real human beings. We began our corporate life in 1977 in an office we shared with a Chevrolet Impala. Today we've outgrown our founding garage but Palo Alto, California, remains Klutz galactic headquarters. For those of you who collect corporate mission statements, here's ours:

Create wonderful things. Be good. **Have fun.**

Write Us

We would love to hear your comments regarding this or any of our books. We have many!

KLUTZ.

450 Lambert Avenue
Palo Alto, CA 94306

Book printed in Korea. Glasses manufactured in Korea.

©2006 Klutz.
All rights reserved.

Published by Klutz, a subsidiary of Scholastic Inc. SCHOLASTIC and associated logos are trademarks and/or registered trademarks of Scholastic Inc. Klutz and associated logos are trademarks and/or registered trademarks of Klutz.

Distributed in the UK by Scholastic UK Ltd., Westfield Road, Southam, Warwickshire, England CV47 0RA

Distributed in Australia by Scholastic Australia Customer Service PO Box 579, Gosford 2250 NSW

ISBN 1-59174-314-1
4 1 5 8 5 7 0 8 8 8

Visit Our Website

Check out all the stuff we make, find a nearby retailer, sign up for a newsletter, e-mail us or just goof around.

KLUTZ.com
Come on in!
OPEN 24 HOURS

You have WEIRD questions.

We have weird answers.

AS THE PROUD OWNER OF A FIRST-CLASS hardly used human body, you no doubt have questions from time to time about how it works. Who wouldn't? Maybe you've lost the owner's manual, or maybe you just want more detailed information.

If so, this is the book for you. It takes a look at vision, a real-life super-power and doubtlessly one of your top five senses. We've written the book in the question-and-answer format and tried to address two kinds of questions. First, the kind that everyone always asks because they're important and second, the kind that nobody asks because they're afraid to, or because they're the kinds of questions that are too weird for normal people to think of. That's where we come in.

We hope you enjoy and learn. And if you think of any questions — even the weird kind — that we *haven't* answered, drop us a card or e-mail us (thefolks@klutz.com) and we'll see if we can't help you out.

Question one
What's so special about this guy?

LOOKING AT THIS photo of a guy in an easy chair we know three things immediately:

1. He's invisible.

2. He's naked.

3. He's blind.

We know he's invisible and we know he's naked for the same obvious reason. But we know he's blind because his eyes are not stopping any light. (NONE of him is stopping any light!) The impact that light makes on the back of your eye (where it is stopped) is transmitted to the brain as a picture.

No impact = no picture = blind as a bat.

This explains why invisible people are so dangerous on the street. You can't see them. And they can't see you.

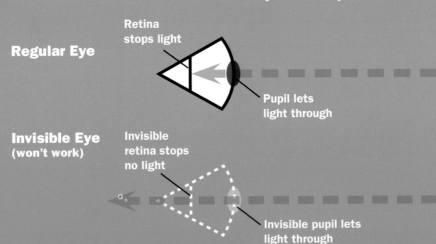

Regular Eye

Retina stops light

Pupil lets light through

Invisible Eye (won't work)

Invisible retina stops no light

Invisible pupil lets light through

Q

uestion two

Is this guy really real?

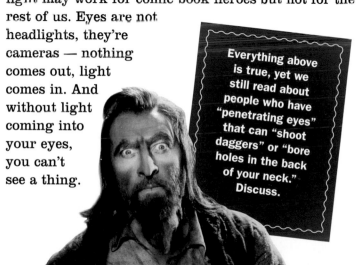

DISAPPOINTINGLY, HE'S NOT. THE IDEA THAT EYES are like marvelous headlights that shoot beams of light may work for comic book heroes but not for the rest of us. Eyes are not headlights, they're cameras — nothing comes out, light comes in. And without light coming into your eyes, you can't see a thing.

Everything above is true, yet we still read about people who have "penetrating eyes" that can "shoot daggers" or "bore holes in the back of your neck." Discuss.

Question three
What really happens when you look at a lady on the phone?

THIS PHOTOGRAPH COUNTS AS ONE OF THE MOST AMAZING science photos ever taken. An extremely tiny camera lens has been inserted into a living eye (that happened to be looking at a lady on the phone) and has taken a picture of the back wall of the eye where the lady's image was being projected. In other words, the camera is pointed into the eye — away from the lady — and is taking a picture of her picture. It's hard to imagine a more dramatic demonstration of how the eye really works than this photograph taken in 1973 by the world famous Lennart Nilsson.

Picture of woman appears on retina

Special camera takes this picture

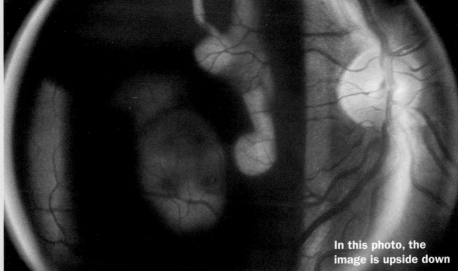

In this photo, the image is upside down

Q | uestion four
What happens when you cross blurred vision with a fad?

THE PICTURE BELOW IS KNOWN OFFICIALLY as a single-image stereogram. If you stare at it while de-focussing your eyes (possible, but not easy), one of two things will happen: Either you'll get dizzy (we do) or the image will "float" up and turn into a clear 3-D picture. When it happens, it's pretty amazing. In 1996, millions upon millions of these pictures could be found on posters and in best-selling books.

Start with your nose against the image and pull back slowly. Try to see through the paper until something comes into focus in the mid-range.

Q

What are the two most vulnerable places on your body?

IN A WORLD FILLED WITH STINGING BUGS, NASTY GERMS, hot stoves, sharp edges, and the occasional spitting snake — your skin is your armor. It is pierced in only a very few places, and only when absolutely necessary.

Two of those piercings are located almost exactly across the mid-line of your face. Millions of years ago predators learned to recognize them as two side-by-side darkish spots. And, just as this cobra is doing here, they learned to direct their attention directly towards them.

With excellent reason. Those two little holes in your face are the weakest points in your skin armor — your eyes. Amazingly, these two little weak spots give you more information about the world than any of your other senses.

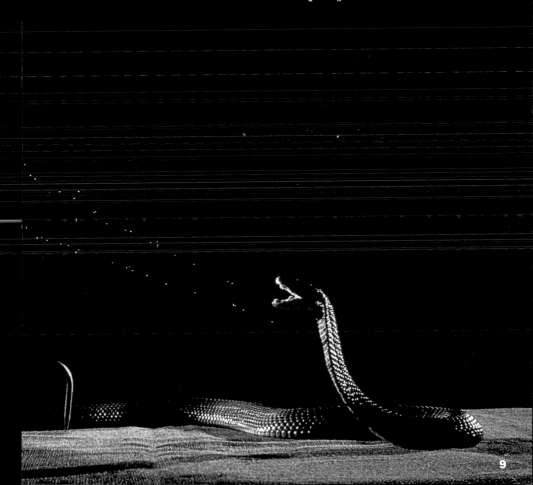

Q | uestion six
One of these pictures is impossible for the human eye to see. Which one?

A.   **B.**   **C.**

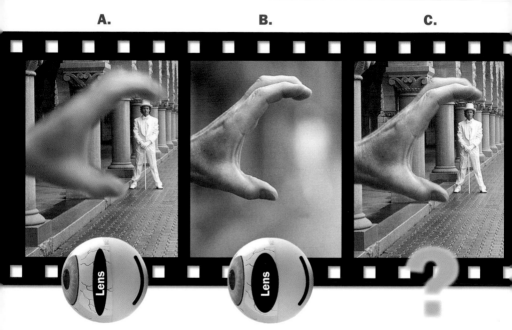

A. When you're looking at the guy, your lens looks like this.

B. When you're looking at your hand, your lens looks like this.

C. When you try to look at both at the same time, you can't.

THE ANSWER IS BEHIND DOOR NUMBER **C.** WHY? Because both the nearby thing and the background thing are in focus. Impossible for the human eye. When you're looking at something nearby, your lens shapes itself for that job. When you're looking at something far away, ditto. One lens cannot make itself into two shapes at the same time. You'll have the same experience with a pair of binoculars. Choose what you want to focus on — you can't have it both ways.

Question seven
How'd we get this kid in the bucket?

CAMERAS OFTEN HAVE LENSES THAT can do a much better job of near and far focussing than eyes. When your eye is looking at a nearby bucket, everything behind the bucket is a blur. But a camera — with a particular lens — can put them both into focus. So you can sometimes get photos of people with telephone poles coming out of their heads, whereas in life, you never see that. Here, we've just lined up a nearby bucket with a faraway kid. Click.

Q | uestion eight
Do animals have glow-in-the-dark eyes?

No. IT WOULD BE CLOSER to the truth to say that animals have mirror eyes. Many animals have a reflective layer called a tapetum at the back of their eyes. A flash from a camera enters the eye, reflects off the tapetum and bounces right back — and shows up in a photo. That's how these alligators in a Florida swamp got their "glow-in-the-dark" eyes.

The tapetum helps animals — especially animals that are active at night — see better. It reflects the little bit of light that's available back to the retina a second time. More light means better vision.

What are your phosphenes?

CLOSE YOUR EYES. Squeeze them tight and rub them a little bit and you'll get your own little light show — white blobs and streaks called "phosphenes." By rubbing on your eyes you set off your light-sensitive neurons. (In other words, you're fooling some neurons into thinking the lights are on.)

Q

Are bats blind as a bat?

No. Bats need their eyes almost as much as you do. But they do have a second ability, called echo-location, that supplements what their eyes can see. It works a bit like radar. The bat sends out a chirping noise which bounces off whatever's around him. If something is nearby, the echo comes back quickly. If it's farther away, it takes a little longer. Somehow, the bat is able to process this echo information and build a mental picture of his surroundings.

Question eleven

Will your eyes get ruined by reading in bad light, and if you cross them, will they get stuck like your parents have always told you?

No AND NO.

Taking a picture in poor light makes for a bad picture, but it doesn't damage the camera. The same is true for your eyes. It's a little tiring to read in bad light, but don't worry — you won't go blind.

As for crossing your eyes, they're no more likely to stick there as anywhere else.

Note: Every time we print these facts, we get letters from people who don't believe them, especially the poor light, ruined eyes story. But they have both been repeatedly confirmed by medical eye specialists. So go ahead! Read in the pitch dark! See if we care!

BONUS FACT!

If you eat a normal diet, extra carrots will not improve your vision.

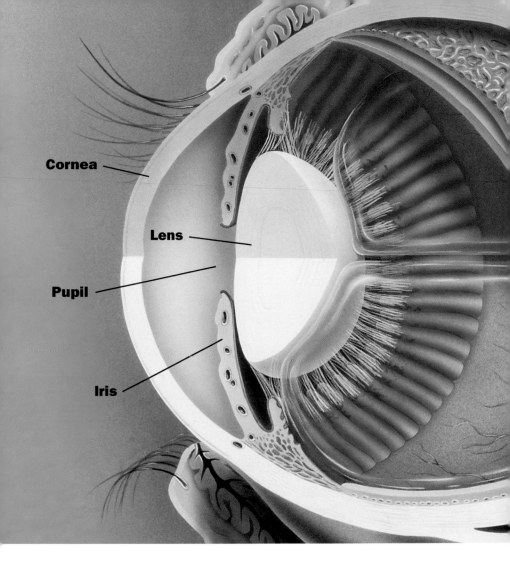

Cornea

Lens

Pupil

Iris

Q | uestion twelve
Do you need lenses to see?

SURPRISINGLY, NO.
Without a lens, you
wouldn't be able to see well
— everything would be out
of focus — but you would
be able to make out large
shapes and movement, a
huge improvement over
absolute blindness.

When the lens clouds
up, as often happens in
old age, it can eventually
cause blindness. Today
the condition is called
cataracts and it's usually
cured quickly with
surgery.

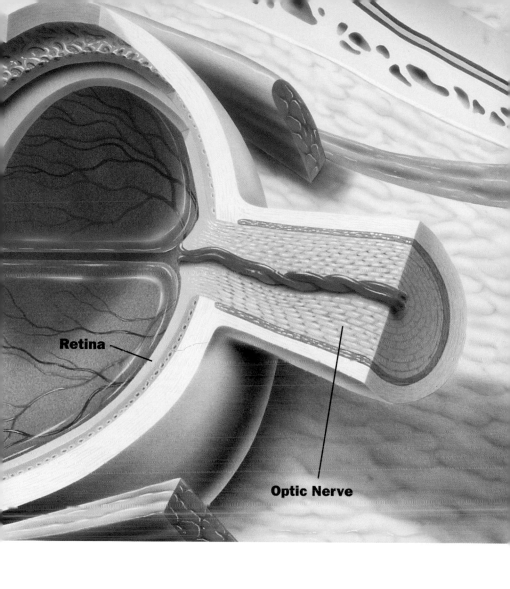

Retina

Optic Nerve

Two thousand years ago, one of the world's first cataract specialists was an Indian surgeon by the name of Sustruta who used a technique called "couching." It went like this: You'd come into his office, lie down, he'd stick a knife in your eye and push the cloudy lens out of the way, then you'd get up and feel your way out.

The amazing thing? Couching actually worked (sometimes). No lens is better than a cloudy lens.

(Want to entertain a really scary thought? In 2000 years kids will be reading about today's doctors and what they did to you. And guess what they're going to think?)

Q | uestion thirteen
Which of these tables is bigger?

WE'RE NOT SAYING because you wouldn't believe us anyway. Measure the table tops.

Question fourteen
Is square A the same color as square B?

A

THEY ARE, ACTUALLY, but you'll have to block out everything in the picture except the squares before you'll believe us.

This phenomenal illusion (created by Dr. R. Beau Lotto) relies on the fact that the brain has a built-in ability (we call it a shadow-correcto machine). A red sweater that you wear all day changes in color every second as you move into and out of shadow. But the brain isn't fooled; it doesn't suddenly start believing in the concept of color-changing sweaters. The brain makes an automatic adjustment (with its shadow-correcto machine) and the sweater stays the same red all day long. When we look at the shaded side of the cube, the shadow-correcto machine kicks into gear. But it misses the fact that the artist pulled a fast one. Square B has not been shaded. **Gotcha!**

B

Question fifteen
Are these wheels moving?

NO. YES. WELL, SORT OF. THEY'RE NOT TURNING because they're actually printed on the page and have no moving parts. But, as you can see, they sure appear to be turning. It's you who is making them turn. Your eye flickers from light to dark space and wheel to wheel, and this eye movement fools your brain into thinking the wheels themselves are moving.

You can also stop the turning by staring at any spot on a wheel for a couple of seconds. But as soon as you look away they're on the move again.

Which guy is the shortest?

WE SET UP THIS SCENE to play a little joke on your brain. You're used to seeing faraway things as small, like the guy at the back of the picture. But seeing small things in the foreground means they're well, small. Years of looking at things has taught you this. When we stuck the small background guy in the foreground, your brain scratched its head and figured he must be the smallest.

Answer
Measure them.

Q | uestion seventeen
Does this man have a jump shot?

No. PIRATES (AND CYCLOPSES TOO, COME to think of it) are uncommon in the NBA because two eyes are the secret to good depth perception. And good depth perception is the secret to throwing a ball into a basket that's far away. If you have two eyes, each eye gets a slightly different view of the hoop — about an inch different is all — but this difference enables your brain to form a 3-D picture.

Since your eyes are only separated by a nose, your ability to perceive depth is a bit limited. However, if your nose were HUGE, that could make a significant difference. So, here's the question: Do basketball players with big noses shoot better than others with normal noses? (If you do a science project on this question, and the associated research, please send it to us immediately. We will print it in the next edition of this book.)

Q | uestion eighteen
Can you identify the predator? And the prey? Just by looking at their eyes?

A.

Predator or Prey?

B.

Predator or Prey?

PICTURE B IS THE DINER (PREDATOR).
PICTURE A IS THE DINNER (PREY).

Predators have eyes facing frontwards for good depth perception (a big help when hunting for dinner).

Prey animals have eyes on their sides of their heads, so they can keep watch for predators sneaking up on them.

Chickens have such far-apart eyes that they can't combine two views into one 3-D view. To overcome this, they jerk their heads from side to side. This jerking motion gives each of their eyes two views of the same thing. Their brains combine the two views into a 3-D image.

Where is your mid-air sausage finger?

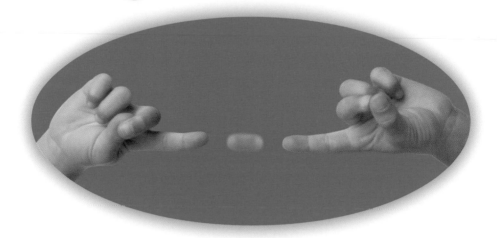

YOU'RE PROBABLY NOT going to believe this unless you try it yourself. Stare at a wall. Hold your pointer fingers about 15 inches (40 cm) in front of your eyes as shown. Bring your fingers together until you see a little sausage finger floating in mid air. So cute! It has two nails and everything. If you close an eye, the finger disappears. Open both eyes and it's back again.

Your eyes are used to seeing two separate images of things, which your brain puts together into one 3-D image. But when you stare past your fingers at the wall, your eyes can't focus on your fingers. Your brain gets a hazy impression that there are fingers there, but it can't combine them into a clear image. The best it can do is to create a bit of overlap from both fingers — the mid-air sausage finger.

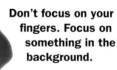

Don't focus on your fingers. Focus on something in the background.

Q | uestion twenty
Are you lefty-eyed?

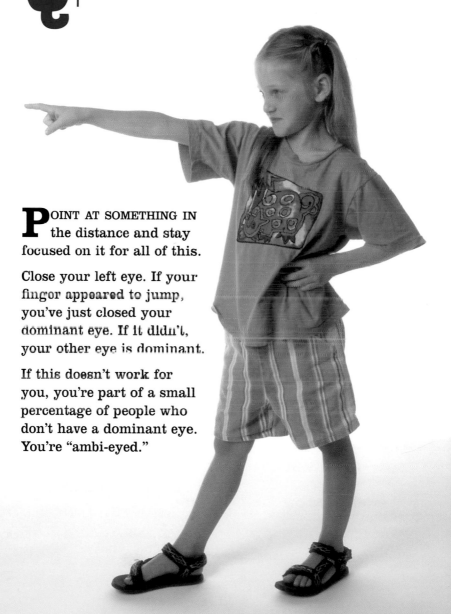

POINT AT SOMETHING IN the distance and stay focused on it for all of this.

Close your left eye. If your finger appeared to jump, you've just closed your dominant eye. If it didn't, your other eye is dominant.

If this doesn't work for you, you're part of a small percentage of people who don't have a dominant eye. You're "ambi-eyed."

Q | uestion twenty-one
Can
you
read

If you can you must be under 40 years of age.

After 40 years of use, the lens in the human

eye loses flexibility, and can't focus well

on small things — like this type.

Q | uestion twenty-two
Where's your
blind sp t?

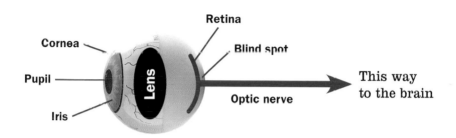

Cornea · Retina

Pupil · Blind spot

Lens

Iris · Optic nerve

This way to the brain

Hold this page at arm's length with your right hand. Close your left eye and look at the . You'll see the out of the corner of your eye. As you look at the , slowly bring the page toward your face. *Very* slowly. Notice when the disappears. Make the reappear by continuing to bring the card toward your face.

The disappears at the point where its image on your retina is exactly on the blind spot, the place where the optic nerve leaves the retina and goes to the brain. You are blind to any image that falls on this spot. You aren't normally aware of your blind spot because your eyes are always moving around. The brain fills in the information that is missing in the blind spot, a tiny area in your field of vision.

Question twenty-three
How come these glasses make these pictures look 3-D?

IT'S A TRICK, JUST LIKE YOU THOUGHT. Here's how it's done.

You take a picture of something. Then you move the camera approximately one nose-width to the left and shoot the same thing again. The first shot is how your right eye would see it, the second shot is how your left eye would.

You print the first shot in red ink only and the second shot in blue ink only — on the same piece of paper. Next, you put on the funny red and blue glasses. With the red eye, you'll see only the blue picture. With the blue eye, the opposite. Two pictures, one nose-width apart. Your brain blends them together to make one 3-D looking picture — just like it always does, not realizing it's a trick.

Q

uestion twenty-four
Why aren't there any purple tigers?

BECAUSE THEY'D STARVE. So would hot-pink cheetahs, safety-orange lions and lime-green leopards. Many large predators — animals who dine on other animals — rely on stealth and speed to get their dinners. Over millions of years, their coats have evolved to look like whatever is usually behind them. It keeps them well-hidden and well-fed. If all the plants of Africa suddenly turned into screaming shades of neon, in a few million years, the leopards and tigers would be lime-green and neon purple.

Question twenty-five
How can I put a hole in my hand?

THERE ARE SEVERAL EXTREMELY painful ways of doing this, but we recommend another approach.

1. Roll a piece of paper into a tube and hold it over one eye. Place your hand up as shown.

2. Keeping both eyes open, stare into the distance through the tube. Presto — instant hole in hand.

What's going on?

The tube makes you see a circular view of the world with one eye. Your other eye sees your hand. Your brain combines the two views into a hand with a big hole in the middle of it.

Credits

Editor:
Valerie Wyatt

Design: Kevin Plottner

Production: Paula Hannigan

Oddball: John Cassidy

Photo Research:
Stephen Forsling